Adult ADHD Starter Guide

The Brutally Honest First Step to Understanding and
Managing Your Neurodivergent Brain

Amy Harper

To my family, whose love is the driving force behind each of my activities, thanks for being my lighthouse through rough seas.

Preface

Dear Reader,

Thank you for choosing "Adult ADHD Starter Guide." It means a lot to me that you're joining me on this journey.

ADHD has been a part of my life since I was a kid. I had my ups and downs for as long as I can remember. And just like you, I've faced many challenges in my professional and personal life.

Despite all the difficulties, I've learned many things. I've spent years trying to make sense of ADHD and figure out how to thrive with it. During my decades working in the field of psychology, I've met and helped so many people like you.

This book isn't made to solve all your ADHD struggles. Its purpose is to honestly address why other solutions might have failed you and how to take your first steps toward a more manageable life.

I hope you achieve your goals!

Amy Harper

Exclusive Offer

Thank you for purchasing this book! Before we get started, I would like you to know that I am committed to helping you thrive with ADHD. Because of that, I am offering you this exclusive offer, which is optional and only complimentary to the contents of this book, in case you want to walk the extra mile.

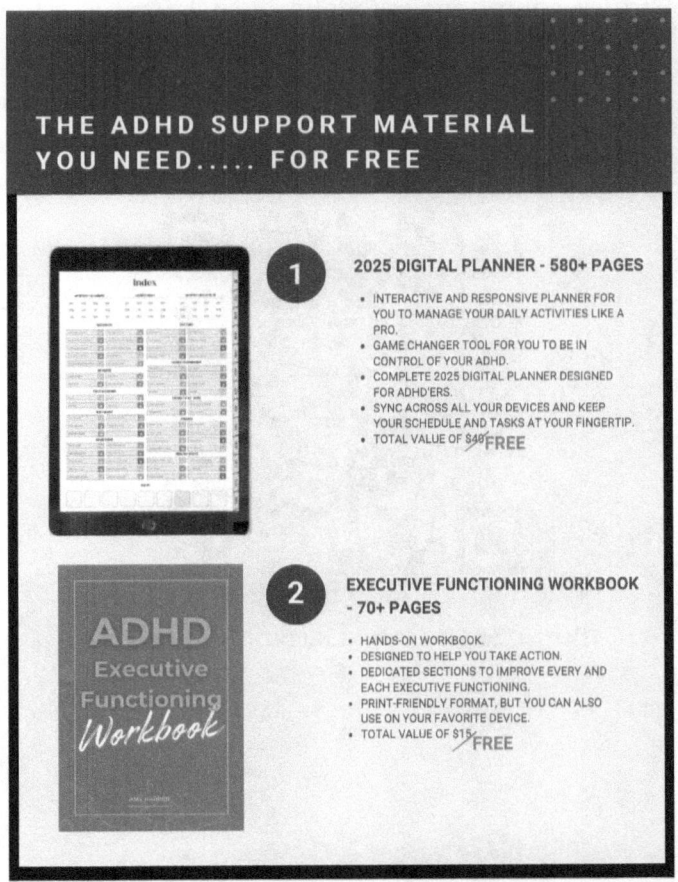

This is what you will have access to:

1) 2025 Digital Planner: This is a responsible planner for you to use in your preferred annotation app. Keep your calendar, to-do lists, checklists, guides, and so much more at your fingertips. It is a tool for your daily use.

2) ADHD Executive Functioning Workbook: I made this workbook to help you improve your executive function skills. It has exercises to find your strengths and weaknesses. You can use the strategies to be more organized and balanced. Working on the exercises will help you progress step by step.

I want you to be equipped and feel confident on the journey you are about to start.

Scan the QR code below to get access to all of them.

(https://amy-harper.kit.com/49acae6b16)

Contents

Introduction

Here We Go... Again

The day Leah had looked forward to for so long had finally arrived: Her children were off at summer camp, her parents out of town, and her husband on the golf course, leaving her with some much-needed alone time. Thrilled by the lack of noise echoing through their family home, Leah made herself a fresh cup of coffee, ignoring the one that went cold hours prior, which she had totally forgotten about. With her coffee in hand, she snuggled into the corner of her favorite couch, ready to jump into her new book on ADHD management techniques for adults. The reviews seemed promising, and she couldn't wait to transform her life as the title promised.

As she dove into the book with great anticipation, a single phrase caught her attention: You don't have to suffer from ADHD; you need to be more organized. Great, Leah thought, rolling her eyes, Here we go again. You see, this wasn't the first book on ADHD Leah had read. In fact, it was one of many. Yet, every book left her wanting more (even if she managed to finish it before tossing it across the room). Truth be told, Leah had started to wonder whether any ADHD book had actually been written by someone with ADHD since most of the advice seemed either too technical and scientific or purely over-simplified and unrealistic. Advice like "just be more organized" was about as helpful as telling a blind person to "just look around."

Perhaps you can relate to Leah? I know I can! I've tossed my fair share of books across the room, frustrated and overwhelmed by advice that seemed more condescending than helpful. But maybe I can provide you with some hope. I can't promise that this book will change your life. I also can't promise that every technique in this book will work for you specifically. But here's what I can promise you:

- I won't provide you with advice that's oversimplified or condescending.

- I'll use science and research to back up my techniques, not use them as the main point.

- I won't sugarcoat things or inspire you with false positivity.

- I'll keep it simple and, well, fun. Life's too short to read a boring book, even if it's self-help.

In proper ADHD fashion, I've told you what the book's about before introducing myself, so let's reverse for a second. My name is Amy Harper; I'm 53 and prefer to live in the woods than in the city. My husband and two daughters are my pride and joy, and I can't imagine my life without my lovable Luna (our golden retriever). I enjoy spending time in nature, board games, and eating cake. But the most important thing you need to know about me is that I have ADHD. Since I can remember, I've known that my brain works a little differently than most of my friends, and while it was daunting at first, it's something I've grown to appreciate and love.

Am I the most organized person you'll ever meet? Not by a long shot. But have I devoted my career to understanding ADHD and crafting methods that are actually effective in managing symptoms? You bet! I like to describe what I do with this image: Imagine you're in a room, busy writing an exam. You want to concentrate, but there's an obnoxious radio playing all your favorite songs (and that one catchy jingle from seven years ago). All you can do is hum along, no matter how hard you try to focus on the test. Well, that's ADHD for you. The methods in this book will not remove the radio from the room. It also won't reveal all the answers to the test. But it will provide you with a remote control that you can use to turn down the volume, perhaps even press pause for a limited time period, and enjoy the freedom of focusing on one task at a time.

So, over the next four chapters, I'll introduce you to the basics of what you'll need to start seeing a difference in your life. This book will not contain all the answers I have because, frankly, that will only overwhelm you. Instead, let's start small, discussing one topic at a time and applying them practically as we go. Consider this book a starting point, not the whole journey. It will provide you with a solid foundation you can use to develop personalized strategies that will actually work. I'm not promising a miracle cure. Instead, I'm promising a start, and it's coming from someone who truly understands where you're coming from.

So, with all the yapping done, are you ready to jump in and possibly make this book your hyperfixation for the next couple of hours? Cool, I'm right there with you. Let's do this!

Chapter 1

I Have It, But I Don't Understand It

When I was fresh out of college, I moved to a new town all on my own. It was the first time in my life I was completely independent. While the freedom was wonderful, it was also very daunting, especially with my ADHD. One area I particularly struggled with was time blindness. I often showed up late for work (or 30 minutes early), unable to figure out how long I needed in the morning to get ready or how to estimate the time it would take me in traffic. One morning, after showing up 10 minutes late for work, my manager called me into their office (understandably). With tears in my eyes, I expressed how much I loved my job and how I was struggling to adjust from student life to a working adult with ADHD.

My manager listened patiently and then asked, "So, what exactly is ADHD? Is it that thing that means you're unorganized and can't sit still?" Wiping my tears and thankful that I still had a job, I answered, "No, it's more than that. It's..." BLANK. I had nothing. I had no idea how to put into words what it was because no one really ever asked me before. Probably because most people assume they know what it is, or at least know the stereotypes. I remember feeling so ashamed of myself. I could already picture the headline: ADHD—I have it, but I don't understand it...

As you can imagine, I spent the rest of that day researching ADHD and how I could put into words what I was experiencing inside my head. In this chapter, we'll discuss my findings (and the findings of the thousands of scientists who actually researched it). So, if you're a little like me, certain you have ADHD but not super sure how exactly it works, I've got you. Let's start by looking at what ADHD is and what it isn't.

> **ADHD Fact:** Some historians speculate that historical figures like Albert Einstein and Thomas Edison might have exhibited traits of ADHD. Their intense focus, creativity, and unconventional thinking align with some of the strengths associated with ADHD (Turner & Smith, 2023).

What It Is (And Isn't)

ADHD is like having a supercharged brain that refuses to focus on the one thing you want it to focus on. It's not a quirk or being lazy—it's a neurodevelopmental disorder. In other words, it affects how your brain develops and works (About Attention-Deficit/Hyperactivity Disorder, n.d.). The ADHD brain is wired a little differently than a neurotypical mind, making it hard to follow patterns created by people without ADHD. While something might seem random to a neurotypical person, it makes perfect sense to someone with ADHD, and vice versa.

There are three main struggles when it comes to ADHD (Inside the ADHD Brain, 2022):

- attention (what did you say?)

- impulse control (add to cart)

- executive function (where did I put my keys again?)

The ADHD mind struggles to focus on one task at a time unless it really piques your interest. If it does catch your attention, chances are you'll focus on that thing only and forget about the rest of the world (oh, hello, cold coffee mug that I forgot to drink three hours ago). Impulse control includes struggling to think before you act. It often manifests as saying something totally out of pocket, which you regret later, or coming home with another rescue animal you don't have space or money for. Lastly, executive function includes things like planning, organizing, and problem-solving. The ADHD mind thrives on structure, but it really struggles to stick to it.

But what exactly is happening in the brain? Well, certain areas of the brain, like the prefrontal cortex, are smaller in individuals with ADHD (ADHD & the Brain, 2017). Why does that matter? Because the prefrontal cortex is in charge of impulse control, focus, and, you guessed it, executive function. The ADHD brain physically looks different from a neurotypical brain, which proves that ADHD is very real and it's not just poor behavior or laziness.

Another big difference between an ADHD mind and a neurotypical mind is the function of neurotransmitters. What are neurotransmitters? Picture them as chemical messengers that help brain cells communicate with each other. Dopamine and norepinephrine are two important neurotransmitters that play a role in ADHD (Neurotransmitters, 2022). Studies suggest that people with ADHD have lower levels of dopamine and norepinephrine, which causes ADHD individuals to do other things that boost dopamine. That's why so many people with ADHD struggle with binge eating and addiction.

> **ADHD Fact:** Brain imaging studies have revealed differences in brain structure and function in people with ADHD. These differences can affect attention, impulsivity, and hyperactivity (Altered Brain Connections in Youth, 2024).

The Myths

Now that we know what ADHD is, we should probably address some of the myths as well. One of the most common myths is that ADHD is just about being hyperactive. While hyperactivity is a common symptom, not everyone with ADHD is a bundle of energy. Some people with ADHD are actually more on the quiet side, often described as "spacey" or "dreamy." That's why so many young girls go undiagnosed for such a long time because they don't display typical ADHD symptoms.

Another myth is that ADHD is caused by bad parenting or sugar. Look, as much as I would love to blame all my struggles on my gummy bears, that's not the case here. ADHD is a neurodevelopmental disorder, meaning it's rooted in how the brain works, not what you had for dinner. Sure, your food plays a role in managing your symptoms, but it's not nearly as big a deal as people make it out to be, and it's most definitely not the cause.

The third myth I want to debunk is the idea that people with ADHD are lazy and unmotivated. This is a huge misconception and can really hurt someone with ADHD (as you probably know well). Individuals with ADHD, more often than not, want to focus and be organized, but their brain works differently. It's like trying to run a marathon with a sprained ankle—hard and slightly impossible, even if you want to.

Lastly, it's crucial to know that ADHD isn't just a childhood disorder. Sure, it can be diagnosed as a child, but it's not something that goes away. As adults, you simply learn how to manage (or mask) it better. The symptoms might even change as you get older, but it won't just disappear.

Key Challenges of an ADHD Brain

Earlier, I mentioned that three of the main struggles of ADHD are attention, impulse control, and executive function. While that's still the case, I want to focus on two key challenges of an ADHD brain, one being executive function. However, I also want to focus on the emotional aspect of ADHD, which includes impulse control. Let's take a closer look at these two key challenges of an ADHD brain to ensure that we fully understand what ADHD is and that it's more than just struggling to focus.

Executive Dysfunction

Imagine your brain is like a browser with 50 open tabs. One of the 50 is blasting music, but you can't seem to find which one it's coming from. Well, that's pretty much what the ADHD brain feels like most of the time. Executive function is the ability to keep your browser tabs organized (or simply close them after you've finished working on that page). For a neurotypical mind, keeping the browser clear and organized comes naturally. Sure, sometimes there might be additional stress or periods of busyness where the tabs can feel overwhelming, but the non-ADHD mind will close the tabs when they are no longer needed and pull up the right ones when the information is required. However, it's not that simple for the ADHD mind as it struggles to know which tabs are still in use and which ones are simply slowing down the processing speed. This leads to four major issues:

- **Time management:** As you might know, the ADHD mind struggles to estimate how long tasks will take, which leads to poor time management and probably a few missed deadlines. Because of all the open tabs, it might underestimate or overestimate the time required to accomplish the task at hand.

- **Task initiation:** The open tabs also make it difficult to start tasks, especially if they're complex or require sustained effort. The ADHD mind already feels overwhelmed, so the thought of starting a project seems impossible at times. The struggle with task initiation is one of the reasons why people with ADHD are often mislabeled as lazy or unmotivated, which actually isn't the case at all.

- **Task completion:** Starting tasks isn't the only struggle the ADHD brain faces—it's equally as difficult to finish tasks. This can be due to losing interest, getting distracted, or simply forgetting that there was a task to complete in the first place.

- **Organization:** The last executive function struggle the ADHD brain might encounter is good old organization. The ADHD mind might struggle to keep track of belongings, appointments, and deadlines, leading to disorganization and forgetfulness. It's important to know that this is not a sign of disinterest or a lack of care.

Emotional Dysregulation

When it comes to emotions in the ADHD mind, it's a little bit like a roller-coaster: one moment you're cruising, the next you're experiencing the high of a dopamine boost, and the next you're falling fast, heading toward a deep slump of despair. Oh, and did I mention that it then starts all over? The ups and downs of the ADHD roller coaster is an endless loop that shoots you high in the sky without warning, followed by a quick and sudden drop. The ADHD mind often experiences intense feelings that feel out of proportion to the situation (Hassall, n.d.). A minor inconvenience can trigger a meltdown, causing a lot of emotional turmoil. This isn't because the person is simply dramatic, but because their hormone levels genuinely jump up and down all the time. This is called emotional regulation and can manifest in a couple of ways:

- **Intense reactions:** The ADHD mind might feel things really deeply, sometimes to the point where it's hard to calm down.

- **Quick mood swings:** Going from happy to sad or angry in a flash is very common for someone with ADHD, and it can be quite exhausting to keep up with your own emotions and make sense of them in real time.

- **Difficulty managing stress:** For the ADHD mind, feeling overwhelmed can occur very easily, and struggling to cope with stressful situations is quite common.

But don't worry; there are lots of strategies to help manage emotional dysregulation (which is what we'll discuss in later chapters and other books in this series). With practice, we can learn to ride that rollercoaster more smoothly!

It's Not a Superpower

When people first hear I have ADHD, it's usually one of two responses:

1. The first one is filled with awkward pity and sounds something like, "Oh no, I'm so sorry. My sister's husband's brother's son also has it."

2. The second one is the unsolicited excitement, which sounds

something like, "That's amazing. You know it's like a superpower, right?"

I must admit I have more patience for the first type of response than I have for the second, probably because the second response diminishes the real struggles of ADHD. Calling it a superpower feels cheap, almost like I'm not allowed to admit that I'm struggling or having an extra hard day because "it's actually a good thing!" And let's face it, if you're falling from a five-story building, would you rather have Superman fly in and save you with his strength and ability to soar through the air, or would you prefer someone who is still searching for their car keys? Yup, it doesn't feel like a superpower anymore, does it?

However, while it's not a superpower if you know how to manage and harness your ADHD, there are some benefits you can enjoy. But these benefits don't take away from the struggles you're experiencing. It's simply a small joy you can embrace in the midst of the chaos. There are two benefits in particular that stand out among most individuals with ADHD: creativity and hyperfocus. Let's take a quick look at each as we finish this chapter on getting to know ADHD a little bit better.

Creativity

According to the Merriam-Webster dictionary, creativity is the ability to create (2019). This includes being able to come up with new ideas, concepts, or solutions. Creativity also involves thinking outside the box, allowing your mind to make connections between seemingly unrelated things. This allows you to approach problems from different angles. People with ADHD often exhibit enhanced creativity due to several factors, including the following:

- Divergent thinking: Instead of seeing something from the same point of view over and over again, someone with ADHD is more likely to generate multiple ideas and perspectives for a single solution. If plan A doesn't work, don't worry—there's already a plan B, C, and D (Jiang & Cho, n.d.).

- Risk-taking: While this can also be a negative thing, in some cases, risk-taking can be considered a benefit. People with ADHD may be more willing to take creative risks and experiment with unconventional approaches, making them more effective in problem-solving and other creative pursuits such as arts and crafts (Kelly, n.d.).

Hyperfocus

Hyperfocus is a state of intense concentration where a person becomes deeply absorbed in a specific task or activity (Flippin, 2024). It's like having a laser beam of focus that shuts out everything else around you. People with ADHD often experience hyperfocus, especially when they're engaged in something they find interesting or stimulating (Ashinoff & Abu-Akel, 2019). When someone with ADHD is in hyperfocus, they can achieve incredible things. Instead of getting bored or distracted after a couple of seconds, they can work for hours without getting tired while still producing high-quality work. But hyperfocus isn't all sunshine and rainbows. It can also make it difficult to switch tasks or take breaks, which can lead to problems with time management and productivity, and it can even lead to burnout and other health concerns (Focus and Organization, 2023).

ADHD Fact: Studies have shown that people with ADHD often possess heightened creativity. Their ability to think differently and approach problems from unique angles can lead to innovative solutions (White, 2019).

Creativity is a very valuable asset for anyone, but when you have ADHD, it can be hard to harness the creativity coursing through your veins effectively. In the next chapter, we'll explore why other solutions you've tried haven't worked yet and what makes this series of books any different. With that being said, give yourself a pat on the back: You've finished the first chapter!

Chapter 2

Am I Doing Something Wrong?

O ver the course of my career, I've worked with hundreds of individuals to manage their ADHD symptoms and live their lives to the fullest. Usually, by the time I meet them, they've tried a handful of other methods with no success. Some might have experienced brief moments of relief in the past but didn't experience long-term success, leading to loads of frustration and shame. One of the first things I ask my clients is what methods they've tried before. The longer the list, the heavier their hearts, and I can feel the shame in their voice. Usually, they ask me the same question: "Am I doing something wrong?"

It breaks my heart every time I hear that question because I've asked it myself many times before. It took me a long time to accept the truth that I wasn't doing anything wrong. If you try to put a small car tire on a large truck and it doesn't work, will you blame the tire or the truck? Well, neither. You'll probably blame the mechanic who told you it's the right size tire. The same goes with ADHD and the techniques we're told to implement to overcome our ADHD. The problem is that most ADHD methods and techniques were created by people who don't have ADHD. So, I want to tell you the same thing I always tell my clients: It's not your fault, and you're not doing something wrong.

Every case of ADHD is different, and just because something might have worked for someone else doesn't mean it has to work for you. Instead of seeing it as a failure, try to see it as another step closer to finding what works for you. With every method and technique you've tried that didn't work, you gathered information to lead you to the methods that will work. In this chapter, we'll first chat about why other solutions don't work, and then we'll explore the emotional toll of repeated failure and what we can do about it. We'll end the chapter by exploring why it's so crucial to look at techniques and tools that are specially designed with the needs of ADHD individuals in mind. So, are you ready to shake off the failures of the past and look to the future? Remember, you're not alone. I've got your back!

Why Other Solutions Don't Work

When other solutions don't work out, it can be quite hard. You might wonder what you're doing wrong or why they don't work, so let's talk about it. The reason why other solutions don't work isn't because you're doing something wrong but because they rely on linear thinking (which isn't the ADHD brain's strong suit). As you might know, neither of those two things is particularly helpful or exciting to anyone with ADHD. For people with ADHD, who tend to think more creatively and flexibly, these tools can feel restrictive and counterproductive instead of helpful and encouraging.

When I was still in school, I used to beg my mom for a beautiful wall calendar and daily planner every year. Usually, this plea of mine was met with resistance. "You're not going to use it," my mom would say, and she wasn't entirely wrong. But each year, I would promise her and myself that I would use it every single day, and for the first week or two, I did! But then I would look at all the days remaining and feel overwhelmed. How am I supposed to keep this up for an entire year? Still, I tried my best. Eventually, I would forget about it for one day and feel like a total failure. Instead of brushing it off as "whatever," I would give up on the idea of using a daily planner completely because I had already failed.

For many ADHD individuals, planners and calendars can feel overwhelming and lead to abandonment after the first few days. Or, they'd simply forget to even look in the calendar. So many times, I've missed appointments scheduled in my physical calendar. For a calendar to work, you actually need to look at it—who knew? So, does that mean all ADHD people should give up on calendars and day planners altogether? Not at all. But it needs to be different than a regular calendar. Here are a few tips that I've found helpful.

- **Digital:** A digital calendar might not be as satisfying as a physical one, but it's more approachable and accessible to people with ADHD. Best of all, it sends you reminders, so you don't even have to look at the calendar to be reminded of your appointments. And let's face it, you're more likely to check your phone every day than you are likely to check your physical calendar. There are hundreds of calendar apps you can use, but you don't even have to use a fancy app if you don't want to. You can use the calendar that comes with your phone. Personally, I enjoy using Google Calendar since it's automatically connected to all my devices.

- **Color:** Color coding is crucial when it comes to making planning tools work for you. I know a monochrome and clean aesthetic is more trendy right now, but what good's a trend if it doesn't work for you? ADHD individuals tend to be visual learners and thinkers (thank you, creative superpower), and you can use that to your advantage by incorporating colors into your calendar. For example, social appointments can be highlighted in pink, while work meetings can be highlighted in blue. Using color is a great way to create borders for your mind so it knows what to expect exactly and what belongs to which activity. You can incorporate color into your digital or physical calendar.

- **Visible:** The final tip for creating a calendar that works for your ADHD mind is to ensure it's visible. Whether it's the first tab that automatically opens when you open your laptop or a large printed sign in the bathroom that says "check your calendar," it's crucial to make visible reminders for yourself. I have a sticker on my mirror that says, "Calendar time!" and every morning, while I brush my teeth, I open my calendar on my phone and check whether there are any important meetings or activities I need to be aware of. Here's the catch, though: You need to switch up the visual reminder. Why? Because your brain will get used to it and eventually start to ignore it. While it might work for non-ADHD minds to have it in the same place for the rest of their lives, your brain needs excitement and change. So, set yourself a reminder every couple of weeks to change your visible prompt.

As you can see, with these small changes, you can change the traditional methods so they work for your ADHD mind. Are you reinventing the wheel? Not at all. You're simply making small adjustments to ensure that the tools you're using actually work for you and won't lead to more frustration and disappointment.

The Emotional Toll of Repeated Failure

Imagine you're trying to build a house, but every tool was created specifically for someone else. The hammer is larger than your entire body, too heavy to even move, and the saw is so small you can use it to file your nails.

How long do you think it will take you to build the house? Probably forever, if I'm being honest. Frustration will build with every swing, every miss, and every misaligned piece. Well, that's exactly what you're experiencing when you're trying to use traditional time management and organizational tools. You're using tools that were created for someone else—tools that won't serve you any good.

As we mentioned, neurotypical tools are very linear and don't allow flexibility and creativity. As a result, you'll feel like a failure. With every missed deadline, it contributes to a sense of inadequacy and a growing belief that you're not capable of managing your own time (or life). But this is more than just a temporary frustration. These constant reminders of your failures can have a huge emotional impact, and it can lead to feelings of shame, anxiety, and depression (ADHD and Stimulation-Seeking Behavior, 2022). No one wants to feel like they're not good enough, and that's why so many ADHD teens tend to give up in school: They're tired of trying and failing, so they become what everyone already thinks they are—lazy and indifferent.

The ADHD brain thrives on novelty and excitement. Traditional tools tend to be repetitive, which can feel like a prison to anyone with ADHD. So, not only are you trying really hard to use the tools given to you and failing, but you're also finding it boring, making the motivation to try again very, very hard. In other words, you're trying to do something that wasn't created for you, even though you find it brain-numbing, and while you're using all your energy to remain engaged, you end up failing anyway. Doesn't sound like a fun time, does it?

You've probably felt like a failure many times before, and because of it, you might be filled with guilt and shame. But let's take a moment to look at this objectively: You're feeling guilty and ashamed because you've failed at thinking and behaving in a way that your body and mind were created to think and behave. In reality, you have nothing to be ashamed of. So, why don't you take a moment and shake the heavy burden of failure and embrace a new perspective? You are here, still going, and still trying to find a way to be better, and that should be celebrated.

To help lighten the load, let's take a look at the need for ADHD-specific approaches and what it means for you and me.

The Need for ADHD-Specific Approaches

Here's the thing: Traditional time management and organization tools aren't terrible. They work for many people and can be beneficial to anyone who is neurotypical. But they'll never work for you, and that's okay. You need techniques and tools that embrace your unique strengths and challenges. We don't have to reinvent the wheel. With small changes to traditional methods, you can go from feeling like a failure to finding tools that are effective and encouraging. Instead of fighting the way the ADHD brain works and trying to force it into a rigid schedule with no flexibility, we need to embrace how the ADHD mind is different from others. Here are three main things to consider when creating an approach.

Flexibility

Intense schedules can be a major source of stress and frustration, which is why you need to create a plan that provides you with moments of spontaneity and novelty. Instead of a strict schedule that you need to stick to, you should embrace the idea of flexibility. Flexibility is crucial for the ADHD brain because it

- **Accommodates spontaneity:** As someone with ADHD, you most likely often experience sudden bursts of energy or unexpected dips. A flexible schedule allows you to capitalize on these moments of productivity and take breaks when needed.

- **Reduce stress and anxiety:** A rigid schedule can create unnecessary pressure. When plans change unexpectedly, a flexible approach can help minimize stress and anxiety.

- **Boosts motivation:** Having a flexible schedule can make tasks more appealing to the ADHD brain. The ability to choose when and how to tackle a task can greatly increase your motivation and productivity, which is a big win in itself.

- **Prevents burnout:** An intensely rigid schedule can very easily lead to burnout for the ADHD mind because it will require so much energy to stick to the schedule. By allowing for flexibility, you can go at your own pace and avoid feeling overwhelmed by everything you have to stick to.

Incorporating flexibility might be daunting, but I believe you'll find it easier than you might think, especially when you start noticing the difference in how it makes you feel. Here are three ways to incorporate flexibility into your daily life instead of having a rigid schedule:

1. **Use time blocking:** Instead of strict time slots in which you have to accomplish specific tasks, take a more relaxed approach and create time blocks. A time slot is a specific time that you have to do something, while a time block is a longer period of time assigned to do various different tasks in whatever order you want to. By using time blocks, you have more flexibility in your schedule.

2. **Learn how to prioritize:** Instead of focusing on doing tasks in

a specific order, begin the day by identifying the most important tasks. Then, choose to focus on completing those tasks first. On the other hand, your less important tasks can be moved around or even postponed if you run out of energy or time. Don't focus on completing everything every single day since this will only add pressure.

3. **Build in buffer time:** Schedule buffer time between tasks to account for unexpected interruptions and changes in plans or to allow your mind to wander where it wants to.

By embracing flexibility, you can create schedules that work for you, reducing stress and increasing overall well-being.

Creativity

Creativity can take the most boring of tasks and transform it into a fun adventure! Similarly, it can turn a rigid schedule into a flexible framework for your ADHD brain. By incorporating creativity into your plans, you can tap into your ADHD brain's unique strengths and make the process more enjoyable and effective. Let's take a look at a few fun ways to add some creativity and magic to your daily schedule.

- **Visualize your goals:** Instead of creating a boring list that inspires no action or excitement, create a visual representation of the tasks at hand. You can use colorful charts, mind maps, or even draw pictures to illustrate your tasks. This is especially helpful if you love to doodle. By visualizing your goals, you can make your plans more engaging and motivating.

- **Experiment with different formats:** Since we know they don't work effectively, don't be afraid to break away from traditional planners and calendars. Instead, try something new and exciting, like digital tools, bullet journals, or even a notebook without dates, so you have loads of space to doodle. Find a format that sparks your creativity and suits your unique style.

- **Incorporate creative breaks:** The best way to incorporate creativity and ensure you're not burning yourself out is by scheduling short breaks throughout your day. Your ADHD mind needs to rest in order to engage in creative activities. Taking short breaks filled with a creative outlet can help you recharge, reduce stress, and boost your productivity. You can try drawing, singing, or even learning a new instrument.

Rewards

Here's a little pro-tip that opened my eyes to a whole new world of understanding: The ADHD brain thrives on immediate gratification and positive reinforcement. How can you capitalize on that knowledge? By incorporating frequent rewards into your schedule. Here's why that works so well:

- **Dopamine boost:** When you receive a reward, it triggers the release of dopamine. Dopamine is a neurotransmitter associated with pleasure and motivation (Dopamine, 2022). When you get a dopamine hit in the middle of your day, it will help you to stay engaged and focused on tasks.

- **Improved task completion:** Frequent rewards also work because they break down large, daunting tasks into smaller, more manageable chunks. It's like cutting a massive steak into smaller pieces, which is easier to digest. Completing each chunk of work can lead to a small reward, which makes the overall process less overwhelming and increases the likelihood of completion.

- **Enhanced self-esteem:** Achieving small goals and receiving positive reinforcement boosts self-confidence and reduces feelings of inadequacy often experienced by individuals with ADHD.

- **Reduced procrastination:** The anticipation of a reward can counteract the tendency to procrastinate. It provides an incentive to start and stay on track.

As you can see, frequent rewards are crucial for the ADHD mind. So, how can we incorporate and use it in our daily lifestyle to boost efficiency? I'm so glad you asked! Let's look at a few ideas to get you started.

1. **Identify rewarding activities:** The first step is to determine what activities you truly enjoy and find motivating. These could be anything from taking a short break to watching a favorite show or indulging in a hobby. It can also include a fun snack or playing with your pet. Whatever you find rewarding, write it down.

2. **Set realistic goals:** Next, you need to break down larger tasks into smaller, achievable steps with milestones. Assign a reward for each milestone or every completed step.

3. **Reward yourself regularly:** It's crucial that you don't wait too long between rewards. Frequent, smaller rewards are often more effective than infrequent, larger ones. So, don't think you have to reward yourself with something huge and expensive. Sometimes, the best reward is allowing your mind to run around without restraints for five minutes or to take a 20-minute nap.

4. **Celebrate milestones:** The last step is to reward yourself for completing larger milestones, such as finishing a project or meet-

ing a long-term goal. These can be larger rewards or something you've wanted for quite some time. Personally, I enjoy taking myself out for dinner after completing a project I've been busy with for a while.

While all of these steps are important and helpful, you have to experiment and find what works best for you. Don't be afraid to try something and then adjust it when it doesn't work. That doesn't mean you're a failure! Embrace your creativity and find a solution that works for you. It doesn't have to work for everyone else as long as you find it helpful. In the next chapter, we'll explore how we can shift the narrative surrounding ADHD from shame to empowerment. You've got this!

Chapter 3

From Embarrassment to Empowerment

Have you ever felt embarrassed by your ADHD? I remember showing up late to a friend's birthday party once, out of breath from running up the stairs, because I thought it would be faster than waiting for the elevator. With sweat forming on my brow, I ran into the room shouting, "Sorry I'm late!" All the eyes turned toward me as someone asked, "No problem, are you okay? What happened?" I wasn't sure what to say. How do I explain that nothing happened physically to make me late but that I was stuck sitting on my bed, wrapped in my towel, doom-scrolling because everything else seemed overwhelming? Embarrassed and desperate to shift the attention elsewhere, I shrugged and said, "Don't worry about it."

I wish I could say that it was an isolated event and something similar didn't happen again a few weeks later, but that would be a lie. However, something did change: my perspective. We spend so much time being embarrassed and ashamed of our ADHD that we never consider the consequences. By being ashamed of something you can't control, you ultimately sentence yourself to a lifetime of pain and struggles. Can you shame your ADHD away? Nope. Can you change your perspective and the way you view your ADHD? Absolutely! So, let's focus on what we can control and watch the magic happen from there. In this chapter, we'll focus on reframing failure. Instead of feeling embarrassed, you'll feel empowered! We'll look at ADHD objectively and find a way to go from being your worst critic to being your biggest fan. Let's jump right in!

Reframing Failure

What does it mean to reframe failure? In short, it's the act of shifting your perspective on failure. It's when you can look at your past missteps and see them as learning opportunities and not doom. Instead of viewing failure as a personal shortcoming or a sign of defeat, you see it as a stepping stone towards growth and improvement. By reframing your failure, you can look at the tools you're trying to use more objectively and with a sense of curiosity.

When you reframe failure, something magical happens. All of a sudden, you focus on the lessons you can learn from the experience instead of getting stuck on the idea that you did something wrong. It allows you to analyze what went wrong, identify areas for improvement, and gain valuable insights, which can then help you avoid making similar mistakes in the future. In other words, you'll go from feeling miserable about the outcome to feeling excited to try again with slight adjustments.

Let's put this into practice, shall we? Think of a previous time management tool you tried and then abandoned. Now ask yourself, why did you stop using it? Instead of seeing it as a failure, take it as a learning opportunity. Was the tool too rigid? Did it overwhelm you? Understanding why it didn't work without self-blame will greatly help you in the future.

Embracing challenges and viewing setbacks as opportunities to learn will encourage you to become more adaptable, and ultimately, you will become more successful in your endeavors. It sounds great, doesn't it? But how can we practically implement it? Is it easier said than done? Let's find out! Here are a few key steps you can take to reframe your failure:

- **Step 1—Acknowledge your ADHD:** It doesn't help to pretend, so start by recognizing that your ADHD can sometimes make it harder to complete tasks or meet deadlines. This isn't a personal failing but a neurological difference. Objectively speaking, it's not personal.

- **Step 2—Break down the failure:** Instead of dwelling on the overall failure, break it down into smaller parts. What specific things went wrong? Understanding the details can help you identify areas for improvement.

- **Step 3—Learn from the experience:** Ask yourself, What can I learn from this? Remember, every failure is an opportunity to gain new insights and develop new strategies. So, instead of dwelling on the defeat, focus on what you can do differently next time.

- **Step 4—Practice self-compassion:** This is probably the most important step. Even if you forget everything else, this is the part you should remember: Be kind to yourself. Everyone makes mistakes. Instead of beating yourself up, offer yourself support and encouragement.

- **Step 5—Set realistic goals:** It's vital that you set yourself up for success by having realistic goals. For example, your goal shouldn't be to become the most organized person in the world, but perhaps it could be to become more organized than you were last week. Instead of overwhelming yourself with unrealistic goals, break them down into smaller, manageable steps.

Remember, failure is not a reflection of your worth as a person. It's a part of the learning process. By reframing failure and focusing on growth, you can build resilience and achieve your goals.

Seeing ADHD Objectively

Seeing ADHD objectively as someone with ADHD is crucial for self-acceptance and personal growth. Instead of viewing yourself as broken, it's essential to recognize that your brain functions differently. We spoke about this at great length in the previous chapter, but it's a good reminder to touch on it again. Understanding your unique strengths and challenges will allow you to find strategies and tools that align with your brain's natural tendencies (Mason & Rosier, 2024).

By reframing ADHD and looking at it objectively, you'll find it easier to be kind to yourself instead of beating yourself over everything you've done wrong. It will allow you to approach your differences with curiosity and resilience instead of shame and embarrassment. When you're curious about your mind, you'll feel encouraged to learn more about it, and the more you know, the better you'll be at finding tools that work for you. There's no one-size-fits-all approach to managing ADHD, and by looking at it from an objective point of view, you're more likely to find solutions that will help you thrive.

To see ADHD objectively can be tricky, especially if you've been told it's "wrong" your entire life. To help you make the change, here are a few tips you can use to see ADHD more objectively.

- **Educate yourself:** Take some time to learn the science behind ADHD, the symptoms, and how it affects the brain. This knowledge can help you understand why certain behaviors or challenges occur.

- **Seek professional diagnosis:** A qualified mental health professional can provide an accurate diagnosis, which can help you understand your specific challenges and strengths. This will help you not to see it as something that's "wrong" with you but simply the way your brain is wired.

- **Recognize your strengths:** When you feel down and frustrated with all the downsides to ADHD, take a moment to focus on the positive traits of ADHD to navigate the difficult parts with more positivity and hope.

- **Understand your limitations:** You don't have to pretend like there aren't challenges. It's important to have a balanced, objective view of the things you're good at as well as the things you're not so good at. This self-awareness will help you to develop strategies to manage your challenges.

- **Practice self-compassion:** Be kind to yourself and avoid self-blame. Remember that ADHD is neurological, not a character flaw.

By taking these steps, you can develop a more objective understanding of ADHD and its impact on your life, which can help you manage your condition effectively and live a fulfilling life.

From Critic to Cheerleader

Kindness is the cornerstone of embracing ADHD with self-compassion. If you want to go from critic to cheerleader, you need to embrace kindness with open arms. Now, that doesn't mean making excuses or taking an easy way out (or blaming poor behavior on your ADHD). Becoming your own cheerleader is about treating yourself with the same understanding and care you would offer your best friend.

How can you achieve that?

By recognizing that these difficulties are a result of your ADHD, not a reflection of your worth as a person. By approaching your struggles with compassion, you can alleviate stress and anxiety, which can further hinder your ability to focus and manage your ADHD symptoms. One of the best tools you can use to transform from critic to cheerleader is affirmations. Affirmations are positive statements that can help rewire your thinking patterns and challenge negative self-talk. By repeating these affirmations regularly, you can gradually shift your perspective and cultivate a more compassionate and understanding attitude towards yourself.

To effectively use affirmations, it's important to choose statements that resonate with you personally. You can write them down, say them out loud, or even record them and listen to them regularly. It's also helpful to pair affirmations with specific actions, such as practicing mindfulness or engaging in self-care activities. I enjoy repeating affirmations as I get ready in the morning. As I wiggle into my jeans, I find joy in my creative mind as I come up with new ways to cheer myself on. Here are a few examples of some affirmations that might be helpful to you.

- My ADHD brain is unique and powerful.

- I am capable of achieving my goals, one step at a time.

- I am learning to manage my ADHD in a way that works for me.

- I am patient with myself as I learn and grow.

- My creativity and energy are valuable assets.

- I am grateful for my ability to think outside the box.

- I am still learning and growing, and it's okay to seek what works for me.

Self-compassion is an ongoing practice and it will take time and practice to see results. By consistently using affirmations and other self-compassion techniques, you can build a stronger foundation of self-love and acceptance. In the next chapter, we'll explore a few practical first steps you can use to enjoy an immediate win, but before we jump ahead, take a moment to repeat a positive affirmation right now. This will set you up for success for our final chapter.

Chapter 4

I Need a Quick Win

With the emotional roller coaster of ADHD, I often find myself feeling down in slumps, unable to move forward. That's when I really need a quick win, a technique or tool I know I can rely on to help me do what needs to get done. In earlier chapters, I mentioned that ADHD isn't a one-size-fits-all approach, so presenting quick wins that will work for everyone is a bit of a struggle, and it's not a guarantee. However, over the years of working with other ADHD individuals, there have been some techniques that stand out and work for the majority of people. These are the techniques I like to call the quick-win tools.

If you've been endlessly trying ADHD methods with no success, I highly suggest you start with these three quick wins. Are they guaranteed to help? Unfortunately not. But are the odds in your favor? One hundred percent! So, in this chapter, I'll present three techniques to you, backed with scientific evidence as to why they work for ADHD minds. But I'll also provide you with some ways to adjust these techniques since flexibility is key. That way, if they don't work for you, you can begin to adjust the different elements of each technique until you find it helpful.

Picture these techniques like one of those fancy massage chairs: You can adjust the temperature, the firmness of the massage, and even the timing until you've found the perfect setting for you. However, to get to the perfect setting, you have to make use of trial and error first. So, are you ready to try these techniques on the factory setting before you begin to adjust them for yourself? Let's do this!

The Two-Minute Rule

The two-minute rule is my go-to approach, and it's one of the first techniques I suggest to anyone who tends to feel overwhelmed quickly. Do you want to know the best part? It's so simple and easy. There aren't any complex steps or philosophical thinking required. All you need is a task that's overwhelming you (or boring you to death) and a timer. Let's say, for example, you've been dreading washing the dishes, and it's overwhelming you by just looking at it. Instead of seeing it as a massive task that you need to accomplish from start to finish, commit two minutes to it. Literally!

Put on a timer with two minutes on the clock, and then wash the dishes until the timer runs out. That's it. Will all the dishes be done? Not at all. But you've started, and that's a win already. Starting is often the hardest part, and you might find that after two minutes, you don't mind to keep going (Cummins, 2024). However, there's no pressure to keep going once the timer has run out. The expectation is not to finish the task but to start.

If you want to make the task more fun, you can also use other ways to time yourself. Personally, I enjoy putting on one of my favorite songs. I commit to working on the task at hand for the duration of the song, and once the song is finished, I stop. After the song, I continue with something else I need to do and then return to the task I struggled with later. Usually, it's easier to return to something that's already started. If it's still challenging, repeat the two-minute rule again and again and again, and eventually, your task will be complete.

You can also modify the rule by extending the working period. If you feel like two minutes is too short, try five minutes or perhaps even ten. This is especially helpful with tasks that require more intense focus, like studying or working. I often find this helpful when I'm writing and set myself a work period of ten minutes at a time. The key lies in making it exciting for yourself. Whether that's why using music as a motivator, making it a competition with yourself to see how far you can come in two minutes, or using a physical timer that runs out, you can keep the core principle of this method and still make it your own.

So, next time you feel paralyzed by a task, why not try this method and see if it works for you? Remember, don't expect a radical change on the first try. You have to customize it to fit your mind, but who knows, it might just be the perfect starting point.

The Visual Approach

Another very helpful approach that I consider a quick win is using color-coding. Have you ever looked at your to-do list and felt completely overwhelmed with no idea where to start? Me too. It's common for the ADHD mind to feel overwhelmed when there's too much to think about (or when there's too little). When you feel overwhelmed by your to-do list, take a moment to make use of color-coding by priority. Here's how:

1. **Choose colors:** Assign colors to different levels of importance. For example, if something needs to get done today, mark it with red. If something needs to get done soon, mark it with yellow, and if something can wait another day or five, mark it with green. You can use whatever colors you want to use as long as they remain consistent.

2. **Evaluate your tasks:** After assigning colors, read through your to-do list and highlight every task with the appropriate color. Be objective about this. Before assigning everything as a top priority, ask yourself: Will something bad happen if I don't accomplish this task today? If the answer is no, it doesn't have to be a red task.

3. **Start:** Once you have your color-coded list, start with the top-priority tasks and take it from there. Remove the not-so-important tasks from your plate to reduce the workload and stress.

4. **Fun tip:** Use another color (your favorite) and reserve it for tasks that you want to do. This can include tasks that you know will boost your dopamine, like unboxing Christmas decorations. Be sure to sandwich a fun task between your red tasks to ensure momentum and prevent burnout.

The visual approach is very helpful for the ADHD mind for various reasons, including

- **Visual clarity:** Colors are visually stimulating and can help your brain quickly identify and prioritize tasks. This can be especially helpful for those struggling with traditional to-do lists (Barrett, 2023).

- **Prioritization at a glance:** By assigning different colors to different priority levels (e.g., red for urgent, yellow for important, and green for low priority), you can easily see what needs to be done first (Smith, 2024). This can help you stay focused and avoid getting overwhelmed by a long list of tasks.

- **Improved focus:** When you can quickly identify the most important tasks, you can focus your attention on them without getting distracted by lower-priority items. This can help you be more productive and efficient (Catchings, 2024).

- **Reduced anxiety:** Knowing what needs to be done and when can help reduce anxiety and stress. Color-coding can help you feel more in control of your tasks and less likely to forget something important (Srinivasan, 2024).

- **Increased Motivation:** Seeing your tasks visually organized and color-coded can be motivating. It can give you a sense of accomplishment as you complete tasks and move them to a lower priority or even cross them off your list.

If you tend to get overwhelmed by your tasks and your to-do list, I highly recommend you try this visual aid quick win and see whether it's a tool that can work for you. Remember, you can make it your own, so use whatever colors you enjoy looking at.

The 5-4-3-2-1 Grounding Technique

The last quick-win technique I want to share with you is a technique to help you regulate your emotions. When you feel like you're stuck on a roller coaster, it can be terrifying. This grounding technique can help you find your calm in the storm and take it from there before you do or say something you'll regret later. The 5-4-3-2-1 grounding technique is a simple but very effective tool for managing overwhelming emotions and bringing yourself back to the present moment (Calm, n.d.). It's one of the first techniques I suggest to others and one I use often. Here's how it works:

1. **Identify five things you see:** Identify five things you can see around you. Focus on the details, like the color of your shirt, the shape of a cloud, or the texture of your skin.

2. **Find four things you can touch:** Name four things you can touch. This could be the chair you're sitting on, the keyboard you're typing on, or your own hands.

3. **Focus on three things you can hear:** Listen for three sounds around you. It could be the ticking of a clock, the sound of traffic outside, or the hum of a computer.

4. **Search for two things you can smell:** Identify two smells in your environment. This could be the scent of your coffee, the smell of food cooking, or the fresh air coming through an open window.

5. **Focus on one thing you can taste:** Notice the taste in your mouth. Is it the flavor of your gum, the aftertaste of your drink, or the natural taste of your saliva?

Engaging your senses in this way will allow you to shift your focus away from overwhelming emotions and unhelpful thoughts and ground yourself in the present moment. Doing so can help reduce anxiety, calm your mind, and bring a sense of peace. However, you don't have to use this technique exactly as I just described it. There are many ways that you can customize it:

- **Simplify:** If you find the original 5-4-3-2-1 format overwhelming, reduce the numbers to 3-2-1 or even 2-1.

- **Prioritize senses:** If you find certain senses more calming than others, focus on those. For example, you might focus on visual and auditory stimuli if you find them particularly grounding.

- **Mindful movement:** A great way to add another layer of stimulation to your grounding is by combining it with simple, mindful movements. This can include movements like stretching, yoga poses, or deep breathing exercises.

- **Sensory motor activities:** If you get distracted easily, try to engage in activities that involve multiple senses, such as drawing, painting, or playing an instrument. This will help you to remain grounded but also allow your mind to be entertained by different activities at the same time.

- **Use a grounding app:** I highly suggest utilizing a grounding app that provides guided exercises and visual aids to help you through the process. This can be especially helpful if you're new to grounding. Some grounding apps you can use include Calm, Headspace, and Smiling Mind.

- **Outdoor grounding:** If you're outdoors, focus on natural elements like trees, flowers, or the sky.

Remember, the key to effective grounding is to find what works best for you. Experiment with different variations of all three of these techniques to find what works for you.

Conclusion

So, What Now?

The day Leah picked up this book, she wasn't very hopeful. She was prepared to be disappointed in yet another book that claimed to understand ADHD, just to be misunderstood again. But to her surprise, she felt seen. Finally, she understood why none of the previous strategies she tried had worked and why her ADHD mind is so different.

Just like Leah, I hope you've found this book helpful. It might have been a short glimpse into the world of ADHD, but I trust that you feel encouraged and understood more than ever before. I hope that you feel inspired to embrace your unique strengths and find techniques you can rely on. It's okay to feel overwhelmed, to make mistakes, and to need a little extra support. The key is to find strategies that work for you. Previous techniques didn't work, and that's okay. It's not because you didn't try hard enough or because you're lazy. Your brain works differently, and that's nothing to be ashamed of. In fact, it should be celebrated! Just imagine how boring the world would've been if we were all the same!

Remember, you're not alone. It might take some time, so be patient and kind to yourself. Keep going, and eventually, you'll begin to find relief in these techniques created by someone with ADHD for someone with ADHD. If you want to learn more, you can also look out for the next books in this series covering other aspects of ADHD. Until next time!

Glossary

ADHD: Attention-Deficit/Hyperactivity Disorder is a neurodevelopmental disorder, and if you're reading this book, it's probably something you've struggled with your whole life. As you might know, it's characterized by persistent patterns of inattention, hyperactivity, and impulsivity. It's not a cute quirk or trend; it's a disorder that can seriously interfere with your daily functioning.

Dopamine: A neurotransmitter in the brain that plays a crucial role in reward-motivated behavior, pleasure, and motivation. It is involved in the brain's reward system, which reinforces behaviors that lead to positive outcomes. Individuals with ADHD may have imbalances in dopamine levels, which can affect their ability to focus, stay motivated, and experience pleasure.

Hyperfixation: A state of intense focus on a particular object, activity, or person. You completely absorb the subject of interest, experiencing a dopamine rush. This often occurs with ADHD individuals, and it can shift very abruptly.

Neurotypical: A term used to describe individuals whose neurological development is considered normal. Most likely includes anyone who ever told you to "just focus" and thought they were being helpful.

Neurodivergent: A term used to describe individuals whose neurological development differs from what is considered typical or neurotypical.

ADHD isn't the only group classified as neurotypical. It also includes people with conditions such as autism spectrum disorder and dyslexia.

Neurodevelopmental disorder: A group of conditions that affect brain development and function. It greatly impacts a person's behavior, learning, and social skills. These disorders typically begin in childhood and can persist throughout a person's life. Examples include autism spectrum disorder, attention-deficit/hyperactivity disorder (ADHD), and intellectual disability.

Time blocking: A time management technique that involves dividing one's day into blocks of time and assigning specific tasks or activities to each block. This can be especially helpful for individuals with ADHD who may struggle with time management and focus.

References

About attention-deficit / hyperactivity disorder (ADHD). (n.d.). CDC. https://www.cdc.gov/adhd/about/index.html

ADHD & the brain. (2017, February). American Academy of Child and Adolescent Psychiatry. https://www.aacap.org/AACAP/Families_and_Youth/Facts_for_Families/FFF-Guide/ADHD_and_the_Brain-121.aspx

ADHD and stimulation-seeking behavior. (2022, August 22). Cross Country. https://www.crosscountry.com/blog/adhd-and-stimulation-seeking-behavior

Altered brain connections in youth with ADHD. (2024, March 25). National Institutes of Health (NIH). https://www.nih.gov/news-events/nih-research-matters/altered-brain-connections-youth-adhd

Ashinoff, B. K., & Abu-Akel, A. (2019). Hyperfocus: The forgotten frontier of attention. *Psychological Research*, *85*(1), 1–19. https://doi.org/10.1007/s00426-019-01245-8

Barrett, S. (2023, November 5). *How colour affects learning: Boosting memory and engagement*. School Planner. https://www.schoolplanner.co.uk/blog/how-colour-affects-learning/

Calm. (n.d.). *5-4-3-2-1 grounding: How to use this simple technique for coping with anxiety*. Calm Blog. https://www.calm.com/blog/5-4-3-2-1-a-simple-exercise-to-calm-the-mind

Catchings, C. V. (2024, April 26). *14 life hacks to help you manage ADHD*. Talkspace. https://www.talkspace.com/mental-health/conditions/articles/adhd-hacks/

Cummins, M. (2024, October 10). *Why ADHD adults have trouble starting tasks*. Marla Cummins. https://marlacummins.com/trouble-starting-tasks-adults-with-adhd/

Flippin, R. (2024, July 10). *Hyperfocus: The ADHD phenomenon of intense fixation*. ADDitude. https://www.additudemag.com/understanding-adhd-hyperfocus/

Focus and organization. (2023, May 2). ADDA - Attention Deficit Disorder Association. https://add.org/adhd-hyperfocus/

Franken, R. E. (2019). *What is creativity?* California State University. https://www.csun.edu/~vcpsy00h/creativity/define.htm

Hassall, J. (n.d.). *Adult ADHD and emotions*. CHADD. https://chadd.org/attention-article/adult-adhd-and-emotions/?utm_source=chatgpt.com

"If you have ADHD, don't try to fit the neurotypical mould," says NOFA ambassador, Phoebe. (2022, October 11). Orchestras for All. https://www.orchestrasforall.org/blog/adhd-dont-try-to-fit-the-neurotypical-mould-national-orchestra-for-all-ambassador-phoebe

Inside the ADHD brain: Structure, function, and chemistry. (2022, December 20). ADDA - Attention Deficit Disorder Association. https://add.org/adhd-brain/

Jiang, Y., & Cho, M. (n.d.). *Is ADHD related to creativity?* CHADD. https://chadd.org/attention-article/is-adhd-related-to-creativity/

Kelly, K. (n.d.). *ADHD and creativity*. Understood. https://www.understood.org/en/articles/adhd-and-creativity-what-you-need-to-know

Mason, O., & Rosier, T. (2024, April 21). *Face it — people with ADHD are wired differently*. ADDitude. https://www.additudemag.com/current-research-on-adhd-breakdown-of-the-adhd-brain/

Merriam-Webster. (2019). *Definition of creativity*. Merriam-Webster. https://www.merriam-webster.com/dictionary/creativity

Neurotransmitters. (2022, March 14). Cleveland Clinic. https://my.clevelandclinic.org/health/articles/22513-neurotransmitters

Smith, M. (2024, November 25). *Tips for managing adult ADHD*. Help Guide. https://www.helpguide.org/mental-health/adhd/managing-adult-adhd

Srinivasan, P. (2024, June 28). *The Eisenhower matrix for prioritization & productivity: A guide*. ClickUp. https://clickup.com/blog/eisenhower-matrix/

Turner, N. E., & Smith, H. H. (2023). Supporting neurodivergent talent: ADHD, autism, and dyslexia in physics and space sciences. *Frontiers in Physics*, *11*. https://doi.org/10.3389/fphy.2023.1223966

White, H. (2019, March 5). *The creativity of ADHD*. Scientific American. https://www.scientificamerican.com/article/the-creativity-of-adhd/

www.ingramcontent.com/pod-product-compliance
Lightning Source LLC
Chambersburg PA
CBHW030519130626
46549CB00007B/3060